Our Planet

Living in a city or in the open countryside, we glimpse only a tiny portion of the Earth's surface, and even that is no more than the outside of a thick skin wrapped around the mighty ball that is our planet. Deep down beneath our feet, the Earth's inside is made of rocks so hot and squashed that certain layers creep and flow like tar. These rocks have shaped the surface of the Earth by building and destroying the ocean floor, pushing continents around, and creating mountains.

The Earth today possesses vast oceans, and great mountain ranges, from which immensely long rivers flow. Its surface varies greatly from place to place, and its many different climates favour different kinds of plants. Underground forces that slowly shift continents and, over millions of years, build mountains, also cause earthquakes and volcanic erruptions which destroy towns and villages in only a few minutes. On the surface, waves, tides and currents continually agitate the sea, and very slowly the levels of the sea and land change. In the atmosphere above us, our weather is formed by the movement of huge masses of warm and cold air.

A stone 'mushroom' sculpted by desert winds.

▼ This diagram shows the sizes of the Sun and planets, and the distances at which these planets orbit around the Sun. The Sun's pull, called gravitation, stops the planets speeding off through space.

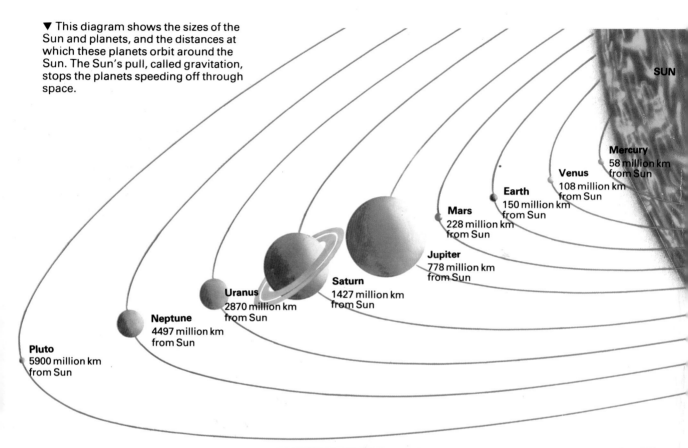

SUN

Mercury
58 million km
from Sun

Venus
108 million km
from Sun

Earth
150 million km
from Sun

Mars
228 million km
from Sun

Jupiter
778 million km
from Sun

Saturn
1427 million km
from Sun

Uranus
2870 million km
from Sun

Neptune
4497 million km
from Sun

Pluto
5900 million km
from Sun

▶ Birds fly in to roost below the setting Sun. From here on Earth the Sun seems small because it is so very far away. In fact it is a giant ball of gas more than a million times larger than the Earth and far hotter than the hottest oven. The Sun constantly beams energy far into space in all directions. It is this energy that lights and warms the surface of our planet and stirs the air and oceans. Without sunshine no rain could fall, no plants could grow, no animals could live. Our world would be a dark, dead, frozen ball. Yet too much sunshine would be just as bad: rocks would melt, seas would turn to steam, plants and animals would bake to death. Luckily the Sun is just far enough away for comfort.

·SUPERBOOK·

OUR PLANET

DAVID LAMBERT

Kingfisher Books

Contents

Kingfisher Books, Grisewood & Dempsey Ltd,
Elsley House, 24–30 Great Titchfield Street,
London W1P 7AD

This revised edition first published in 1986 by Kingfisher
Books. Originally published in large format hardcover by
Galley Press in 1981 as Planet Earth in the Picture Facts
series.

10 9 8 7 6 5 4 3

© Grisewood & Dempsey Limited 1981, 1986

BRITISH LIBRARY CATALOGUING IN PUBLICATION DATA
Lambert, David, 1932–
   The superbook of our planet
   2nd ed.—(King pins)
   1. Earth—Juvenile literature
   I. Title
   850   QE29

   ISBN 0-86272-195-4

Cover design by Terry Woodley
Cover illustration by Janos Marffy, Jillian Burgess Illustrations
Typeset by Southern Positives and Negatives (SPAN), Lingfield, Surrey
Printed in Hong Kong

Previous page: Mont St Michel, a granite
island off the coast of Brittany, France.

in Space ———————————————

The planet Earth is rather like a mighty ball, about 40,000 km (25,000 miles) around. It speeds through space around the Sun at about 30 km per second (18·5 miles per second). Each year on Earth lasts 365¼ days – the time taken by the Earth to complete one orbit around the Sun.

As it travels the Earth spins about its axis – an imaginary line through the Earth's centre – once every 24 hours. The ends of the axis are places at opposite ends of the Earth. We call these places the north pole and south pole. Half way between the poles lies the equator – an imaginary circle around the Earth dividing it into two equal halves or hemispheres. The position of any place north or south of the equator is called its latitude. The tropics are warm places in latitudes close to the equator. Cold polar regions lie around the poles.

Models show the world divided into 360 equal parts by lines of longitude drawn on the surface between the poles. The longitude of any place is its position east or west of the line of longitude that crosses Greenwich in England.

DAY AND NIGHT

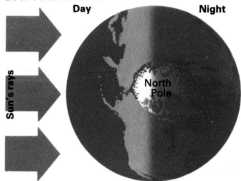

▲ If you could gaze upon the Earth from above the North Pole you would see the Sun's rays lighting one side of our planet. There, it is daytime. The side hidden from the Sun lies in the shadow cast by the Earth. That side of the Earth is in the darkness we call night. The Earth spins with an eastward motion, and takes 24 hours to complete one full turn. This is why the Sun seems to rise in the east and set in the west.

The Seasons

The Earth travels around the Sun tilted at an angle. About June 21 this tilt brings the northern hemisphere closest to the Sun and here, in the north, it is the longest day and the first day of summer. But the southern hemisphere is tilted at its farthest from the Sun so here in the south it is the shortest day and the start of winter. About December 21 the Earth's tilt and the seasons are reversed. About March 21 and September 23 day and night are equal everywhere and spring or autumn starts.

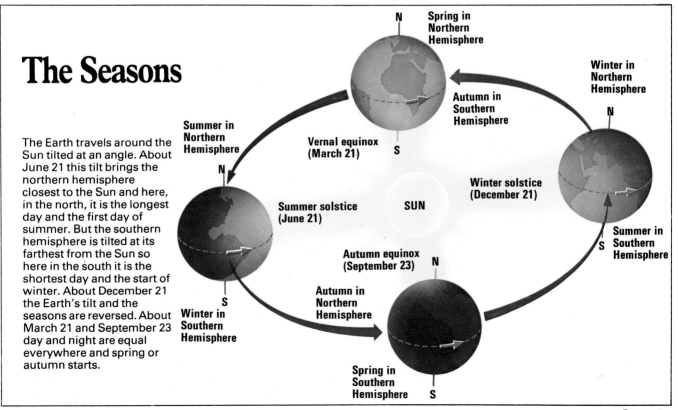

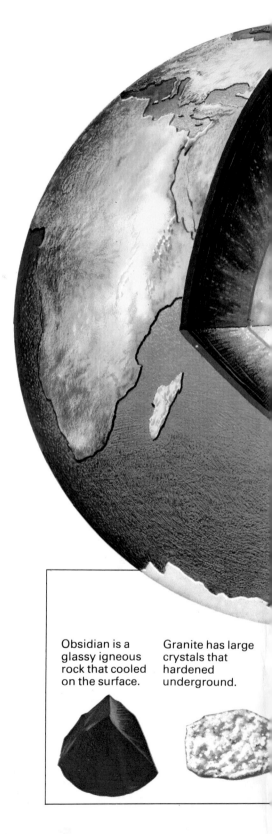

SIZING UP THE EARTH

Inner core: A solid metal ball 2440 km (1540 miles) across, at 3700°C (6700°F) and under a pressure of 3800 tonnes per sq cm (24,000 tons per sq in).

Outer core: A molten metal layer 2240 km (1400 miles) thick. The outer core is mostly iron and nickel.

Mantle: A dense hot layer of rock about 2800 km (1800 miles) thick. Parts are soft and flow like tar.

Crust: The thin outer layer of the Earth. Its solid rocks form a layer about 30 km (19 miles) thick below big mountain chains, but no more than about 6 km (4 miles) thick below the floors of the oceans.

Circumference: 40,075 km (24,902 miles) around the equator; 40,007 km (24,859 miles) around the poles.

Diameter: 12,756 km (7926 miles) across the equator but 12,714 km (7900 miles) between the poles.

Surface area: 510,066,000 sq km (196,935,000 sq miles).

Mass: 5976 million million million tonnes.

Shape: Like a ball slightly flattened at the poles and bulging at the equator.

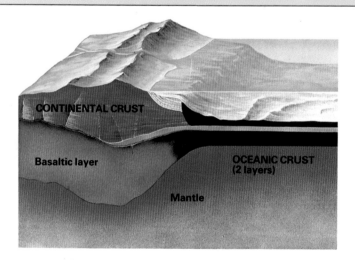

CONTINENTAL CRUST

Basaltic layer

OCEANIC CRUST
(2 layers)

Mantle

▲ This slice cut through the Earth's crust shows the differences between the rocks that lie on land and underneath the ocean floor. Oceanic crust is much thinner than the crust of the continents. Oceanic crust forms simple layers. Continental crust is much more complicated. It is also lighter. But both kinds of crust are lighter than the rocks of the mantle, so they float upon it rather as a cork will float on water.

Obsidian is a glassy igneous rock that cooled on the surface.

Granite has large crystals that hardened underground.

Structure

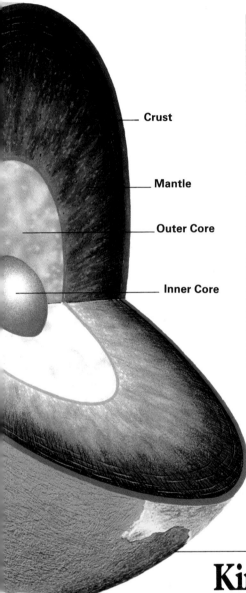

Crust

Mantle

Outer Core

Inner Core

People used to think the Earth has always been the way it is today. Scientists now know otherwise. They believe that our planet began with a great cloud of dust and gas whirling around the Sun. The cloud shrank as its particles drew close together. By 4600 million years ago the cloud had shrunk to form an almost molten planet. Light substances floated up from deep inside to lie upon its fiery surface. There, they cooled and hardened. So the Earth gradually gained the skin of solid rock that makes up most of the Earth's crust.

Meanwhile even lighter substances inside the Earth floated up above the crust and formed an atmosphere of gases.

As the atmosphere cooled down, steam that it contained turned to rain. For countless thousands of years a heavy downpour fell and filled great basins in the crust. So oceans formed.

The great heat locked inside the Earth still disturbs its crust from time to time and helps to push up mountains. But the rain that falls upon the land runs downhill to the sea in rivers, and this flowing water gnaws away the hills.

In one place or another the surface of our world is always slowly rising or being worn away.

▼ Below are eight kinds of rock found in the Earth's crust. Each was formed in one of three main ways. Igneous or 'fiery' rocks like obsidian and granite come from molten rock pushed up from deep down. Sedimentary rocks like coal, limestone, sandstone and conglomerate are made of sediments. These are particles that settled and formed hard layers, usually under water. Igneous or sedimentary rocks changed by heat or pressure become metamorphic rocks, like marble and slate.

Kinds of Rock

Marble is a metamorphic rock formed when heat altered limestone.

Slate is shale changed by heat and pressure into metamorphic rock.

Coal is the crushed remains of prehistoric forest plants.

Limestone comes from thick seabed deposits, mainly of calcium carbonate.

Sandstone is mostly made of grains of quartz from igneous rock.

Conglomerate is natural concrete containing pebbles stuck together.

AGES OF THE EARTH

Era, Period, Epoch	Years Ago
Pre-Cambrian time (life begins)	4600-590 million
Palaeozoic era (fish, amphibians and reptiles appear)	590-248 million
Cambrian Period	590-505 million
Ordovician Period	505-440 million
Silurian Period	440-408 million
Devonian Period	408-360 million
Carboniferous Period	360-286 million
Permian Period	286-248 million
Mesozoic era (age of dinosaurs)	248-65 million
Triassic Period	248-213 million
Jurassic Period	213-144 million
Cretaceous Period	144-65 million
Cenozoic era (age of mammals)	65-0 million
Tertiary Period	65-2 million
Palaeocene Epoch	65-55 million
Eocene Epoch	55-38 million
Oligocene Epoch	38-25 million
Miocene Epoch	25-5 million
Pliocene Epoch	5-2 million
Quaternary Period	2-0 million
Pleistocene Epoch	2 million-10,000
Holocene Epoch	10,000-0

▼ This slab cut from the Earth's crust shows how currents of hot and cooler rock inside the mantle have moved continents and created and destroyed the ocean floor. Currents that separate (1) pull apart the ocean floor above them and plug the gap with molten rock that builds an underwater mountain chain. Colliding currents (2) crush continents together. Their crumpled rocks form mountains. A cooling, sinking current (3) dives beneath a continent, dragging the ocean floor with it.

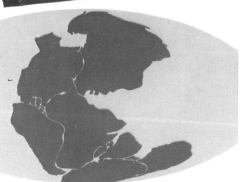

200 million years ago

▲ The world probably looked like this 200 million years ago. All the continents lay jammed close together to form one mighty mass of land. Geographers have called it Pangaea, which means 'all Earth'. India lay wedged between Africa and Antarctica. South America, Africa, Antarctica and Australia were touching one another.

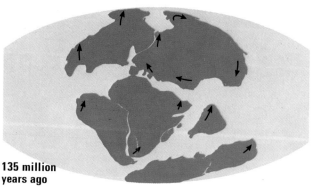

135 million years ago

▲ By 135 million years ago Pangaea began breaking up as continents slowly drifted apart. For a while there may have been two mighty continents. North America, Europe and most of Asia formed one northern continent called Laurasia. South America, Africa, India, Antarctica and Australia formed a southern continent: Gondwanaland.

the Earth

▼ Volcanoes (4) erupt where light, molten rock pushes upward through the crust and escapes on the surface. Earthquakes shake the land where one slab of crust slides jerkily against another slab of crust (5).

▶ The Americas, Africa and Europe would fit like pieces of a jigsaw puzzle if you could cut around them along an underwater line 1000 m (3300 ft) below the level of the sea. Discoveries like this made scientists realize that continents now far apart had once been joined.

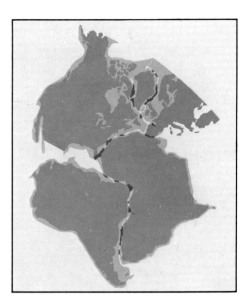

65 million years ago

▲ By 65 million years ago continents may have drifted into these positions. South America became a giant island. India was drifting north towards Asia. But Europe, Asia and North America were still perhaps connected. At the same time Antarctica and Australia may have only just begun to draw apart from each other.

Today

▲ This is how the world is now. A narrow corridor of land joins North and South America. India has crashed into Asia. But an ocean separates North America from Europe, and Antarctica and Australia are island continents. Some time in the future Australia and North and South America may all collide with Asia.

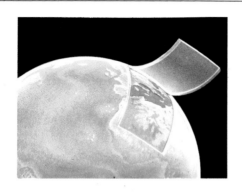

Earth is surrounded by an atmosphere of gases. Only its lowest layer has enough air for us to breathe.

The Atmosphere

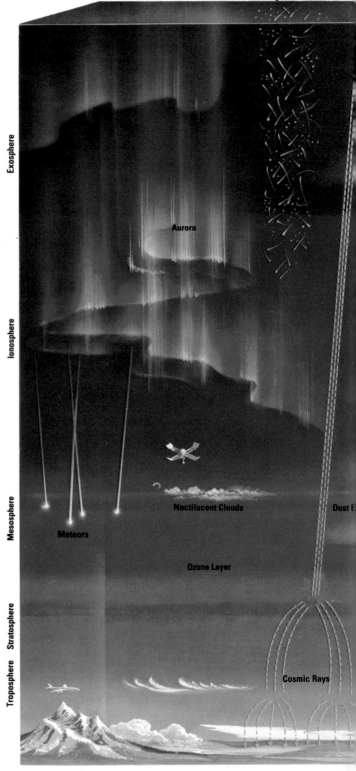

▶ Earth's atmosphere is a mixture of gases floating above the Earth's surface. Earth's pull, called gravity, stops all but the very lightest gases escaping into space. Five main layers make up the atmosphere. From top to bottom these layers are the exosphere, ionosphere, mesosphere, stratosphere and troposphere.

The **exosphere** begins about 500 km (300 miles) above the Earth and stretches far out into space. It is mostly made of the two lightest of all gases, hydrogen and helium. Their particles are very few and far between.

The **ionosphere** is an atmospheric layer 80-500 km (50-300 miles) high. Much of it is ionized (charged electrically) by rays bombarding it from space. Its lower level is a chilly −80°C (−112°F) but higher up the temperature rises until it reaches a sizzling 1200°C (2200°F) at the top. The ionosphere makes long-distance radio possible on Earth by bouncing back radio signals.

The **mesosphere** is about 50-80 km (30-50 miles) high. Temperature falls as height increases.

The **stratosphere** begins 10-18 km (6-11 miles) high and ends 50 km (30 miles) up. Low down its temperature is a chilly −55°C (−67°F). Higher up is a warmer layer rich in ozone gas heated by the Sun. Temperature rises to as much as 10°C (50°F) at the top of the stratosphere. But even in the very lowest levels of this atmospheric layer the air would be too thin for anyone to breathe.

The **troposphere** is only 8 km (5 miles) thick above the poles but 18 km (10 miles) thick above the equator. This is the lowest, densest layer of the atmosphere. In the troposphere winds blow, clouds form and rain falls. The lower levels have enough air for plants and animals to breathe. But air grows thinner and colder as you rise up through the troposphere. Air pressure 18 km (10 miles) high is only one-tenth sea-level air pressure. Also temperature drops by 6°C (11°F) for each kilometre by which you rise above the Earth.

Exosphere

Ionosphere

Mesosphere

Stratosphere

Troposphere

Charged Solar Particles

Aurora

Noctilucent Clouds

Dust

Meteors

Ozone Layer

Cosmic Rays

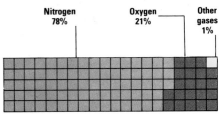

Nitrogen 78%	Oxygen 21%	Other gases 1%

The oxygen we need for breathing makes up only a small part of the air around us. Air is mostly made of nitrogen gas.

◀ **Charged solar particles** are electrically charged particles from the Sun. Many shoot out into space from huge, fiery tongues of molten gas that leap up from the Sun's surface from time to time. Solar particles reaching Earth may affect the weather.

◀ The **auroras** are coloured lights seen in polar skies when streams of charged solar particles attracted to the Earth's magnetic poles collide with molecules of air in the ionosphere.

Noctilucent clouds occur in the stratosphere. They are probably dust from meteors that broke up when they hit the Earth's atmosphere.

The **dust belt** is a band made of particles of dust produced by meteors.

Meteors are also called shooting stars. They are particles from space that burn and glow as they plunge into the atmosphere about 100 km (62 miles) up.

Ozone is a type of oxygen gas. The ozone forms a thin layer that starts about 26 km (16 miles) above the Earth. It absorbs harmful rays from the Sun and warms the stratosphere.

Cosmic rays are particles that shoot through space almost as fast as light. Cosmic rays that reach the stratosphere tend to hit particles of air. These accidents produce weaker rays that shower down upon the surface of the Earth.

Short Waves
Medium Waves
Long Waves

MAJOR WIND BELTS

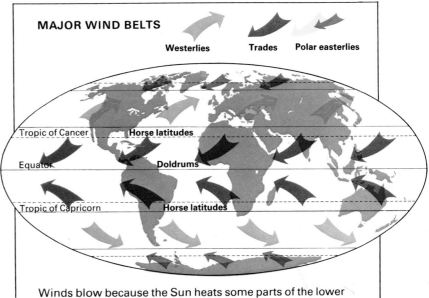

Westerlies   Trades   Polar easterlies

Tropic of Cancer   Horse latitudes

Equator   Doldrums

Tropic of Capricorn   Horse latitudes

Winds blow because the Sun heats some parts of the lower atmosphere more than others. Near the equator, hot air rises from the still regions called the doldrums. This air flows north and south from the equator. Then it cools and sinks in the horse latitudes. From here, some air flows back towards the equator. But some flows towards the polar regions, where it meets and mixes with much colder air flowing outward from the poles. The Earth's spin tends to tug all winds aside.

WAVELENGTHS AND THE ATMOSPHERE

Different layers of the atmosphere bounce back to Earth radio waves of different length. Short waves travel higher than long waves. They are better than long waves for long-distance broadcasting. The shorter the wavelength, the higher the frequency in kilocycles (kc).

Wavelengths	Atmospheric layer reached
Below 500 kc	D layer: 50 km (30 miles) high
500-1500 kc	E layer: 95 km (60 miles) high
1500-30,000 kc (by day)	F1 layer: 200 km (125 miles) high
1500-30,000 kc (by night)	F2 layer: 280 km (175 miles) high
Very short wavelength (UHF)	Penetrates all layers

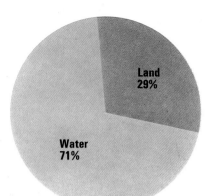

Sizing up the Oceans

▲ If you could put together all the land and all the sea, you would realize that the surface of the world is mostly ocean. In fact water covers nearly three-quarters of our planet.

▼ This diagram shows the different elements contained in seawater. Scientists calculate that there are about 35 tonnes of dissolved salts in every 1000 tonnes of seawater.

Arctic Ocean
Surface area
14,350,000 sq km
Average depth 990 m
Greatest depth 4600 m

Indian Ocean
Surface area
73,490,000 sq km
Average depth 3890 m
Greatest depth 7450 m

Atlantic Ocean
Surface area
106,000,000 sq km
Average depth 3330 m
Greatest depth 9144 m

Pacific Ocean
Surface area
181,000,000 sq km
Average depth 4280 m
Greatest depth 11,022 m

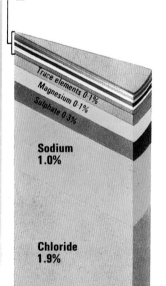

Calcium
Potassium
Bicarbonate
Strontium
Fluoride
Boron
Bromide } 0·1%

Trace elements 0·1%
Magnesium 0·1%
Sulphate 0·3%

Water
96.5%

Sodium
1.0%

Chloride
1.9%

FACTS ABOUT SEAS

Oceans contain about 1300 million cu km (312 cu miles) of water. This is more than 97 per cent of all the water on the surface of the Earth. Oceans take up three-fifths of the northern hemisphere and more than four-fifths of the southern hemisphere. The Pacific Ocean – the largest ocean – is bigger than all the continents put together.

The oceans are always losing water. Each year about 330,000 cu km (80,000 cu miles) of seawater evaporates into the air. Over a quarter of this falls on the land as rain, sleet or snow. The rest falls back into the oceans. Ocean water is always on the move, but one particle could take 5000 years to move through all the oceans.

Oceans

▶ Two diagrams show different ocean depths. Above the continental shelf that rims most continents, the average depth of water is only about 180 m (600 ft). From this shelf a slope leads down to an abyssal plain more than 3000 m (10,000 ft) deep. This plain stands high above the deep ocean trenches. If you lowered the world's highest mountain into the deepest trench, its peak would still be far below the ocean surface.

AND OCEANS

Some seas have far hotter water than others. The Persian Gulf can reach 36°C (97°F) in summer. But parts of the Arctic Ocean are never warmer than −2°C (28°F), the temperature at which seawater freezes. Average ocean temperature is 4°C (39°F).

Seawater is far saltier in some places than others. Parts of the Red Sea have 256 tonnes of salt in every 1000 tonnes of water and tend to buoy up submarines that try to dive. The Baltic is the least salty sea. Parts have only 2 tonnes of salts in 1000 tonnes of water.

PLUMBING THE DEPTHS

Mountains and valleys make the ocean floor uneven. If you could level it, it would be 3550 m (11,650 ft) deep. But the deepest trench, the Mariana Trench in the Pacific Ocean, is three times deeper than that. An iron ball dropped in the sea above would take over an hour to sink to the bottom of it.

Much of the deep ocean floor is carpeted with soft ooze built of the remains of tiny dead plants and animals that drifted down from the surface. Building a layer of ooze 2·5 cm (1 inch) thick takes as long as 20,000 years.

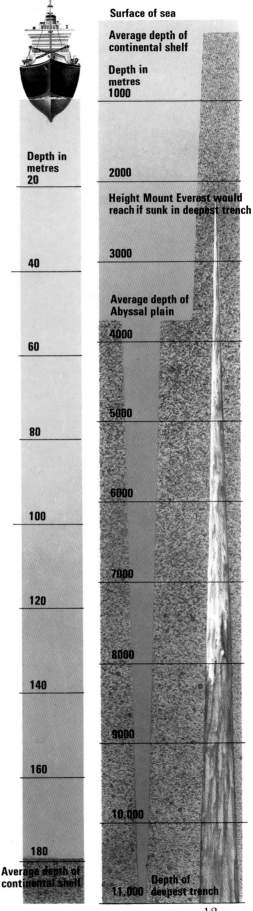

Depth in metres
20
40
60
80
100
120
140
160
180

Average depth of continental shelf

Surface of sea

Average depth of continental shelf

Depth in metres
1000
2000

Height Mount Everest would reach if sunk in deepest trench

3000

Average depth of Abyssal plain
4000
5000
6000
7000
8000
9000
10,000
11,000

Depth of deepest trench

▲ The mighty Himalayas rise from the plains of India like a row of steps. Snow always lies upon the highest, coldest peaks. Scientists think the Himalayas formed after India began crashing into the rest of Asia about 50 million years ago. The crash crumpled up the rocks that lay between India and Asia, much as a flat table-cloth might wrinkle when you push it from both ends.

FACTS ABOUT

Much of the world is mountainous. Seen from space, the highest mountain ranges are no more than low wrinkles on the surface of our planet. But powerful forces went to make the world's great mountain chains and ranges. Most mountains were pushed up when one slab of the Earth's crust met another. *Fold mountains* like the Alps and Himalayas rose when one slab of crust collided with another slab, buckling the rocks between them. The Rocky Mountains and the Andes have grown up where the edge of the Americas meets and rides up above slabs of crust forming part of the Pacific Ocean floor.

When one slab of crust shifts against another, chunks of land may get forced up as *block mountains*.

In places, molten rock from deep down in the crust escapes and piles up on the surface to build *volcanic mountains*.

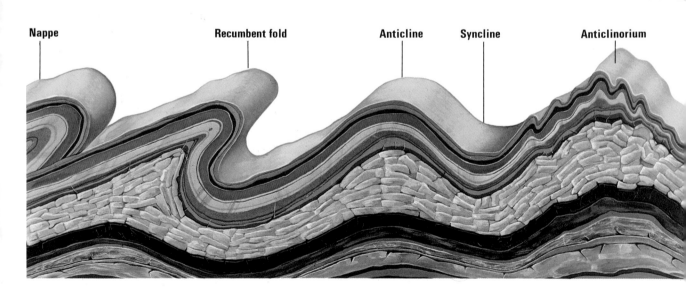

Nappe   **Recumbent fold**   **Anticline**   **Syncline**   **Anticlinorium**

Nappe
This is a layered mass of rock that has been folded far enough to topple over to one side. Then it has slid several kilometres so that it covers other rocks. *Nappe* is a French word meaning table-cloth.

Recumbent Fold
This is a layered mass of rock which has been folded so far that it has toppled over to one side. Recumbent folds and nappes help to build such mountains as the Alps and Scottish Highlands.

Anticline
This is a mass of rock layers (strata) pushed up into a hump by sideways pressure. A big anticline containing small folds is an anticlinorium. There are many in Scotland's Southern Uplands.

Syncline
Synclines are downward folded rock strata. A syncline usually shows as a dip in the surface. But if it gets pushed up, or if the rocks around get worn away, it may become a mountain.

Ranges

▲ Mount Fuji is the highest mountain in Japan, 3776 m (12,389 ft) above sea level. This perfect cone was formed when a volcano poured molten rock onto the surface of the Earth. As the rock cooled it hardened and piled up until it built a mountain peak. The Japanese hold Mount Fuji sacred. Every summer tens of thousands of pilgrims trudge uphill to the summit.

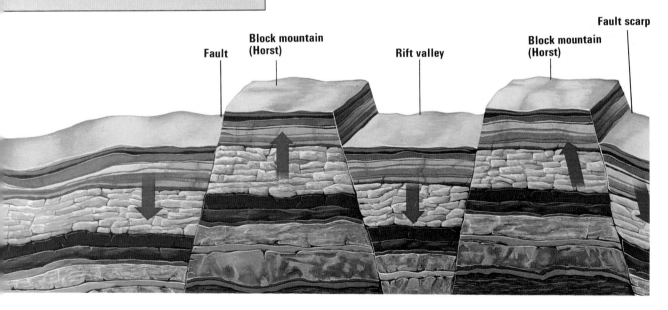

Fault
Faults are breaks in the Earth's crust. The rocks on one side of a fault may move up, down or sideways against rocks on the other side. So rock layers on both sides no longer match each other.

Block Mountain
A block mountain is a mountain formed between two faults. Either the land between the faults rose or the land outside them sank. The Vosges and Black Forest mountains are block mountains.

Rift Valley
This is a strip of land that sinks between two parallel faults. The rift valley system between Syria in Asia and Mozambique in Africa runs almost one-eighth of the way around the world.

Fault Scarp
This is a cliff or steep slope produced when a fault has shifted a mass of land up or down against another mass of land. The Pennine Fault in England is just one example of such a fault scarp.

15

RIVER FACTS

The world's rivers hold about 230,000 cubic km (55,000 cubic miles) of water.

Largest river: Amazon. Each second it pours 120,000 cubic metres (143,000 cubic yards) of water into the ocean.

Longest river: Nile. It measures about 6670 km (4145 miles).

Speeds of different loads borne by rivers: Sand at 0·5 kph (0·3 mph); gravel at 1·2 kph (0·75 mph); big stones at 10 kph (6 mph); boulders at 32 kph (20 mph).

Weight of soil, rock, etc removed by rivers: About 140 tonnes per year from each square kilometre (0·39 square miles) of the Earth's crust.

Thickness of land worn away by rivers: About 30 cm (1 ft) in 9,000 years, as estimated for the United States.

Deepest gorges cut by rivers: Gorges more than 5 km (3 miles) deep made by the rivers Indus, Brahmaputra and Ganges.

Largest delta created by a river: The Ganges-Brahmaputra delta, 75,000 sq km (30,000 sq miles).

Largest area drained by one river system: Amazon Basin, 7 million sq km (2·7 million sq miles).

WATERFALLS

◀ Waterfalls may form if a river flows steeply downhill. The stones it shifts wear away the river bed. If this is made of soft and hard rock layers, the soft layers wear away faster than the hard ones.

Highest waterfall: Angel Falls, Venezuela, 979 m (3212 ft) with a sheer drop of 807 km (2648 ft).

Largest waterfall: Sete Quedas (Guairá), Brazil and Paraguay, 13,000 cubic metres per second (470,000 cu ft per second).

Rivers

▼ Many a river starts as a small stream flowing from a mountain lake fed by melting water from a glacier. Stones shifted by the young river rub against its bed and help to cut a zig-zag valley in the mountain. Where the river crosses hard rock its valley may become a narrow gorge.

Downstream, this river has worn away the hills and flows in giant loops across a gently sloping plain. Here and there it cuts across a loop and leaves it stranded as a curved lake. Near the sea the now sluggish river drops the mud it has been carrying. The mud piles up and slowly builds new land out into the sea. The river may split in two or more to form a delta.

▲ The Colorado River flows through the bottom of the Grand Canyon in Arizona. The Grand Canyon is the world's largest gorge and stretches nearly 350 km (about 217 miles).

17

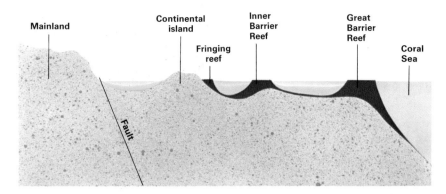

Mainland · Continental island · Fringing reef · Inner Barrier Reef · Great Barrier Reef · Coral Sea · Fault

▲ This slice across Australia's Great Barrier Reef shows how two kinds of islands may form. First, the platform of land right of the fault seems to have slipped slowly downwards. Parts of the sunken land have remained above water, forming islands. Islands that used to form part of a continent are known as continental islands.

As other parts of the land platform sank they gained a covering of coral – a hard, limy, rock-like substance made by tiny sea beasts and certain seaweeds. The coral grew upwards in shallow water until it reached the surface. It shows up at low tide as a string of low coral islands 2000 km (1250 miles) long – the world's longest reef.

Mont St Michel stands in shallow water near Brittany in north-west France. The island's granite rocks are similar to rocks found on the nearby mainland. So Mont St Michel is a continental island, just like the much larger continental islands of Ireland and Great Britain.

▲ White Island is a volcanic island in the ocean off New Zealand. Volcanic islands are mostly shaped as cones and rise steeply from the sea. Many thousand oceanic islands were made by volcanoes that grew from the ocean floor. Some rose 5000 m (16,000 ft) before they broke the surface of the sea. A volcanic island may be born wherever a weak place in the ocean floor lets molten rock escape from deep down in the Earth's crust. Long lines of weakness in the ocean floor help to produce long rows of volcanic islands. The Aleutian Islands of the North Pacific stretch for 1900 km (1200 miles).

▲ The low blue-green band is a coral reef growing around volcanic Raiatea Island. In time the volcanic island may sink beneath the waves while the coral could grow upwards. If this happens, only a ring of coral will remain to show where the volcanic island stood. Such low coral islands are called atolls. The Pacific Ocean has thousands of them.

ISLAND FACTS

Largest island continent: Antarctica, 13,600 million sq km (5250 million sq miles).

Largest island: Greenland, 2,175,000 sq km (840,000 sq miles).

Largest group of islands: Indonesia, with more than 13,000 islands spread across 5600 km (3500 miles) of sea.

▼ Heron Island is a cay or key off the north-east coast of Australia. Cays are low islands built of loose materials, usually sand. The sea piles up sand until the sand forms a low ridge or mound above the waves. Land plants can take root. But storm waves sweeping across the cay may rip the plants out again.

FACTS ABOUT CLIMATE

Hottest places on Earth: Parts of the tropics, regions that lie on either side of the equator. Dallol in northern Ethiopia has an annual mean temperature of about 34°C (94°F).

Coldest places on Earth: Parts of the polar regions in the far north and south. The Pole of Cold in Antarctica has an annual mean temperature of about −58°C (−72°F).

Wettest places on Earth: The rainy tropics. Tutunendo, Colombia, has a mean annual rainfall of 11,770mm (463 inches).

Driest places on Earth: Tropical and other deserts. Part of the Atacama Desert in Chile has no rain for years on end.

Places with the greatest temperature range: Parts of northeastern Siberia in the Soviet Union. At Verkhoyansk the temperature has varied from −70°C to 37°C (−94°F to 98°F), a range of about 107°C (192°F).

Places with the smallest temperature range: Certain regions near the equator. Some islands in the Pacific Ocean have a temperature range of about 12°C (21.6°F).

▲ Palm trees thrive in this rainy tropical climate. In such climates the temperature averages more than 18°C (64°F) in every month, and there is never frost or snow to kill off tender vegetation.

▼ The Sun's rays shine directly down on places near the equator, but shine only slantingly on places near the poles. Also the rays must travel through more air to reach the poles than to reach the equator. So the equator receives more concentrated sunshine than the poles. This is why polar lands have cold climates and tropical lands (lands near the equator) have hot climates.

But warm winds and ocean currents take heat from tropical regions towards the polar regions. At the same time, cold winds and ocean currents from polar regions flow toward the tropics. Where cold air and water meet and mix with warm air and water, places have temperate climates – climates that are neither hot nor cold.

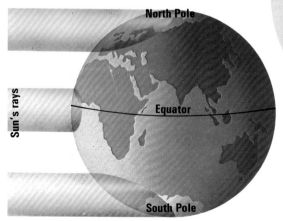

Arctic Circle

Tropic of Cancer

Equator

Tropic of Capricorn

Antarctic Circle

North Pole

Sun's rays

Equator

South Pole

Land

▲ Lush pasture and trees that are about to shed their leaves for winter show that this is a temperate climate. In such climates the average winter temperature is below 6°C (43°F).

Different regions of our world are bathed in sun, drenched by rain, swept by winds, or locked in ice and snow. Each different climatic region has the kind of soils, plants and animals that thrive best in just that kind of climate. Between them, soils and climates create the four main natural regions of the world that are shown in the next few pages.

Great forests sprawl over several continents. Forests of one kind or another can thrive wherever it is moist and warm enough for trees to grow. The world's enormous deserts have formed where the land is too dry for all but scattered, hardy plants. Vast grasslands flourish where it tends to be too dry for trees, but moister than the deserts. Here – and where forests have been cut down – are the world's great farmlands. Lastly, in the far north and south are the chilly polar lands and seas.

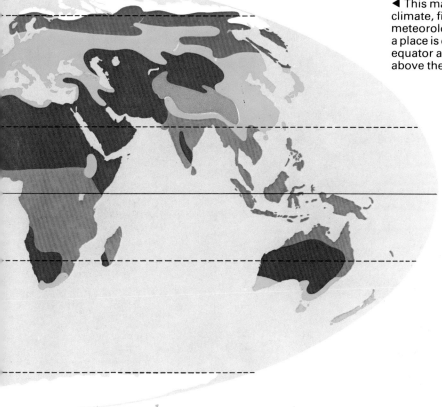

◄ This map shows the world's six main types of climate, first described by the Russian meteorologist Vladimir Köppen. How hot or rainy a place is depends largely on how far it is from the equator and an ocean, and how high it stands above the level of the sea.

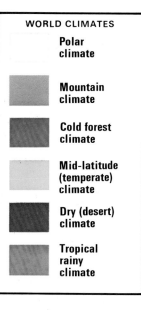

WORLD CLIMATES

- **Polar climate**
- **Mountain climate**
- **Cold forest climate**
- **Mid-latitude (temperate) climate**
- **Dry (desert) climate**
- **Tropical rainy climate**

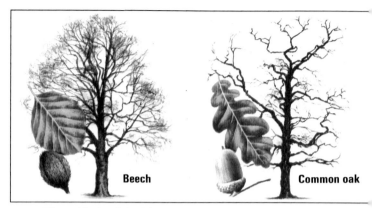

▲ Three kinds of deciduous hardwood trees. Deciduous trees drop their leaves in autumn. This helps to protect the trees from damage caused by snow or winter gales. It also means there are no leaves to lose water in winter when tree roots cannot replace the water from cold or frozen soil.

▲ A tropical rain forest has three main levels. Shrubs, climbing plants, tree seedlings, moss and fungi sprout from the forest floor. High above, a mass of touching tree tops forms the canopy. Here and there, the tallest trees rise above the canopy to form the highest layer. Even a small patch of forest has scores of kinds of tree.

▼ Forest of some kind covers almost one-fifth of the land. Tropical hardwood trees like mahogany thrive where it is hot. But the hardwoods like oak, ash and beech grow in temperate climates. Softwoods such as many pines and firs do best in cool northern lands and on mountainsides. Some regions have a mixture of softwoods and hardwoods.

WORLD FORESTS

Softwoods   Hardwoods   Mixed hard and softwood   Tropical softwoods

(Many of our forests are disappearing fast as trees are cut down and forest lands are cleared.)

and Trees

▼ Giant sequoias in western North America. Rather similar but smaller softwood trees form a great belt of northern forest called the taiga. Unlike the hardwoods, these softwoods bear seeds in cones. Conifers (cone bearers) have tough needle-like leaves that can survive winter cold and winds and a triangular shape that allows the snow to slide off. A huge area of taiga may consist of only one or two kinds of conifer.

Ash

▼ Two coniferous softwood trees, the Scots pine and the larch.

Scots pine

Larch

Deserts

▶ Strange stone 'mushrooms' in the Sahara Desert show where the wind has picked up grains of sand and hurled them just above the ground. Over the years, billions of sand grains have hit the bottom of these mounds, rubbing solid rock away.

▼ This stretch of stones was once one mass of solid rock. Hot days and cold nights caused the outer layers of rock to stretch and shrink slightly. This set up strains within the rock. Bits flaked off. In time the solid surface of the land broke up.

FACTS ABOUT DESERTS

Deserts are dry lands with little rain and few plants. There are hot and temperate deserts. Some people call polar regions cold deserts for most water there is frozen. The four largest deserts are:

Sahara Desert: A hot desert that stretches across northern Africa and covers 8·4 million sq km (3·25 million sq miles). It is almost as large as Brazil, the world's fifth-largest nation.
Australian Desert: A hot desert covering about one fifth of Australia. It measures about 1·5 million sq km (600,000 sq miles).
Arabian Desert: A hot desert covering more than one third of the Arabian Peninsula. It measures 1·3 million sq km (500,000 sq miles).
Gobi Desert: A temperate desert in central Asia. It occupies 1 million sq km (400,000 sq miles).

Sand Dunes

▼ Many deserts have shifting sandy mounds called dunes. They are formed and moved by wind. If wind blows from one direction, loose sand grains lodge against a rock or bush and build a tiny hump. As more sand piles up against it the hillock grows. Wind blows sand up its gentle windward side, over the crest, and down the steep leeward side. In this way a dune may travel forward.

◀ This is a barchan – a dune shaped like a crescent moon. The wind blows its edges ahead of its middle so that the edges curve forward like a cow's horns. If wind blows from opposite directions in different seasons, the horns swing round too. Many barchans grow more than 30 m (100 ft) high. They often form clusters. A row may join to form a long seif dune with dips and ridges. Some seif dunes stretch hundreds of kilometres.

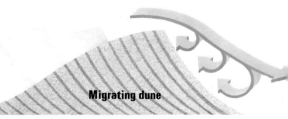

Direction of wind

Stationary dune

Migrating dune

and Sand————

Kinds of Grassland

Much of the world's grass flourishes on land that seems too dry for trees yet suitable for short-lived or shallow-rooted plants.

African Savanna: Tropical grasslands north and south of Africa's tropical forests. The grass grows tall in the rainy season, then dies. Trees stand here and there.

Llanos and Campos: Tropical grasslands (savanna) found in South America. The *llanos* lie north of the tropical forests; the *campos* lie south of the tropical forests. Both are much like the African savanna.

Mountain pastures: Flowery grassland above the highest levels where trees grow.

Prairies: Temperate grasslands of the treeless plains in central North America.

Pampas: Grassy treeless plains in south-eastern South America; like the prairies.

Steppes: Grassy, treeless plains in south-eastern Europe and south-west Siberia; like the prairies.

Veld: Mountain grasslands in South Africa. Some parts are treeless like the prairies. Others include scrub-covered hills.

GRASSLAND SOILS

This diagram shows slices through the soil beneath three kinds of grassland. All grass needs the dark food substance *humus.* North America's dark brown prairie soil and Russia's black chernozem soil have humus near the surface where the shallow-rooted grass can find the nourishment it needs. Chestnut brown soil holds humus too. But it receives less rain than chernozem or prairie soils. So only short grasses and tough shrubs grow well on chestnut brown soils. There are chestnut brown soils in south-east Europe and parts of the United States, Argentina and South Africa.

PRAIRIE SOIL   CHERNOZEM SOIL   CHESTNUT BROWN SOIL

◀ A mounted shepherd rounds up a flock of sheep in open pastureland. Wild sheep graze in mountain meadows, but when sheep were domesticated they were brought down to graze upon the open plains. Now you can see sheep on pampas, steppes and other kinds of temperate grassland all around the world. Australia and New Zealand alone have enough grass for over 200 million sheep. This is about ten sheep for every human being in those lands, and 1 in 5 of all domesticated sheep on Earth.

Wheat

▼ This park-like scene shows part of the *llanos*, the savanna grasslands of northern South America. In the dry season, grasses wither and turn brown, and large parts of the land are parched. But when the rainy season comes, huge tracts of land are flooded. The palm trees in this photograph flourish on a patch of swampy land where the soil is always wet enough for trees to suck up moisture. In tropical grassland, trees are numerous where rain is plentiful. But only drought-proof plants grow in drier areas. Some tropical grasses are very tall: elephant grass can reach 4·6 m (15 ft) high.

▲ Cattle ranching flourishes on many open ranges where a long dry spell each year leaves grasses parched and dead. But it takes a huge area of such thin, poor pasture to keep one cow alive. If the next rains do not come, no new grass grows, and whole herds may starve to death or die of thirst. Most kinds of cattle do best on lusher, greener pasture. Altogether, the world's grasslands feed more than 1000 million cattle.

▼ Combine harvesters gathering a grain crop in the Mid-West of the United States. Farmers now raise wheat where prairie grasses used to grow. Indeed most of the wild prairies have been tamed and changed like this. Much of those other temperate grasslands, the steppes and pampas, have also been ploughed up for growing crops. Short-rooted cereals like wheat and barley thrive upon these soils. This is because these crops are simply cultivated grasses and need the same kinds of soil as the wild grasses that they have replaced.

ARTIFICIAL GRASSLANDS

For centuries farmers in Europe, Asia and North America have been clearing forests and largely replacing them with cereals or pasture.

In the last few years ranchers have chopped down or burnt huge tracts of tropical forest in Brazil. Now cattle graze where monkeys used to swing from tree to tree.

Some people even believe that most of the world's great grasslands are artificial. They think prehistoric people began burning forests thousands of years ago to make extra grazing land for the big wild beasts they hunted.

▼ The Arctic and Antarctic are cold regions of the far north and south. The Arctic is ocean almost surrounded by land. The Antarctic is land surrounded by ocean. Inside the Arctic and Antarctic Circles the Sun does not rise at least one day a year.

At the north and south poles winter darkness lasts for months. In the long, bitter winters, sea and land are frozen. Ice and snow start to melt in summer in the Arctic, but Antarctica never thaws. Most of this mountainous continent lies buried by a sheet of ice larger than the United States and up to 4 km (2·5 miles) thick.

Ice and

ANTARCTIC

Antarctic Circle

South Pole

ARCTIC

Antarctic Convergence

North Pole

Greenland

Arctic Circle

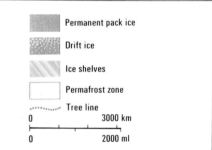

	Permanent pack ice
	Drift ice
	Ice shelves
	Permafrost zone
··········	Tree line

| 0 | | 3000 km |
| 0 | | 2000 ml |

▲ These maps show how and where ice affects land and sea in the polar regions.
Pack ice is a jammed mass of blocks of ice that formed on the sea.
Drift ice is blocks of ice that drift with ocean currents far beyond the pack ice.
Ice shelves are thick, solid sheets of ice jutting from the land far out into the sea.
Permafrost is ground that is always frozen, even where the surface of the soil may thaw in summer.
The *tree line* is the limit reached by trees. The dotted line around Antarctica shows the limit reached by polar ocean water.

◀ A great glacier flows down to the sea somewhere in Alaska. Glaciers are rivers of ice. Many of them lie in polar mountain valleys. If a glacier ends in the sea, great chunks of ice may break off from its snout and drift away as icebergs.

Snow

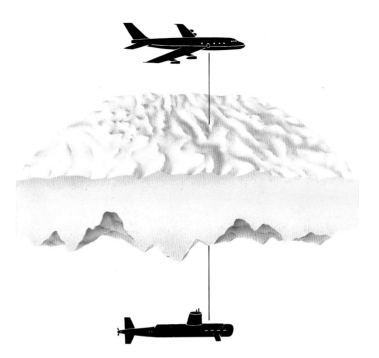

FACTS ABOUT ICE

Ice covers more than one tenth of all the land on Earth at any given time.

Largest ice sheet: Antarctic Ice Sheet, 12·7 million sq km (5 million sq miles).

Longest glacier: Lambert-Fisher Ice Passage in Antarctica. It stretches 500 km (over 300 miles).

Largest ice shelf: Ross Barrier in the Antarctic, 520,000 sq km (200,000 sq miles): larger than Spain.

Largest iceberg: A tabular Antarctic iceberg, 31,000 sq km (12,000 sq miles). This iceberg was larger than Belgium.

▼ Flat-topped, high-sided icebergs like this one break off from the great ice shelves that jut out from Antarctica. The icebergs that break off from Arctic glaciers are narrower, with rugged tops.

▲ A plane flying over sea ice can tell its thickness with help from an instrument known as a laser profilometer. Beneath the ice, a submarine uses an echo-sounding device to get a similar result. Between two-thirds and three-quarters of the thickness of sea ice lies below the water. The tallest iceberg known rose 167 m (550 ft) out of the water. This means that the bottom of that iceberg may have been 500 m (1640 ft) below the level of the sea. The Ross Barrier off Antarctica is believed to measure 400 m (1300 ft) from top to bottom.

Forces acting from underneath and above the Earth's crust help to keep the land, sea and air in motion.

The great heat produced by nuclear reactions deep inside the Earth triggers earthquakes and sets volcanoes erupting. Both occur where the Earth's crust is at its weakest – along the edges of the so-called crustal plates. The Earth's crust is made up of more than a dozen of these giant interlocking 'jigsaw pieces'. Some chiefly go to make up continents. Others form the floors of oceans.

Shifts in the Earth's crust can also raise or lower the level of the land or sea.

The sea itself is stirred about by winds, the Sun's heat, the spinning of the Earth, and the pulling forces exerted by the Moon and Sun. Between them these produce the ocean currents, waves and tides.

The Sun's heat and the Earth's spin produce the winds that blow and help to brew our planet's weather.

San Andreas Fault

Great Valley

Earthquakes

FAMOUS EARTHQUAKES

Shensi Province, China, 1556: Over 800,000 people perished – perhaps more than in any other earthquake.

Lisbon, Portugal, 1755: About 60,000 people died and shocks were felt as far away as Norway.

San Francisco, USA, 1906: An earthquake and the fires it caused destroyed the city.

Kwanto Plain, Japan, 1923: Some 570,000 buildings collapsed. This was the costliest earthquake ever as measured by damage to property.

Lebu, Chile, 1977: The strongest earthquake shock ever recorded.

◀ More than 2000 people died in 1975 when the ground shook and smashed the Turkish town of Lice. The earthquake happened because Lice stands where two of the Earth's crustal plates meet and move.

Earth

▶ Huge holes half swallowed houses when an earthquake struck Alaska in 1964. The earthquake shock sent a wave 67 m (220 ft) high careering through the sea. Special instruments that measure the vibrations set up in the ground by earthquakes showed that this was one of severest earthquakes ever known. It happened at a place where the sea floor is sliding underneath the coast of North America.

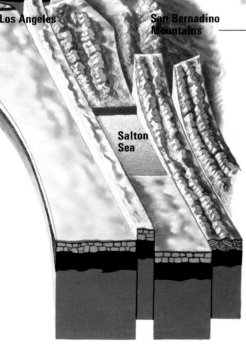

Sierra Nevada

Mojave Desert

Los Angeles

San Bernadino Mountains

Salton Sea

PLATES AND FAULTS

▶ Sometimes two of the vast plates making up the Earth's crust jerk sideways in opposite directions. The sudden movement unleashes an earthquake along the crack in the Earth's crust where both plates meet. Such cracks are called transform faults.

◀ This block diagram helps to show that much of California is made of masses of rock that have been shifted up or down or along against other blocks of rock. The crustal plate west of the San Andreas Fault tries to travel northwest but gets forced westward by the Sierra Nevada Mountains. This helps to trigger earthquakes along the fault. Many thousands of mainly weak tremors have happened this century alone.

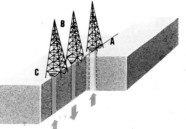

▶ Deep wells sunk along the San Andreas Fault might stop big earthquakes. Here, water is being pumped from wells **A** and **C**. This should lock the transform fault because removing water from it will make both sides tend to jam against each other.

The water being pumped into well **B** should lubricate or 'grease' the fault, letting the rocks on each side slip past each other easily with no more than a very gentle tremor.

▼ (1) Magma (underground molten rock) escapes through a vent (2) to build a volcanic cone (3) of ash and lava layers. Magma cooling underground hardens into slanting dykes (4), level sills (5) and domes called batholiths (6). Magma heats underground water, forming geysers (7). (8) is lava flowing from a crack in the ground. (9) is a lake in the crater of an extinct (dead) or dormant volcano.

Kinds of Volcano

▲ Ash showered far and wide when the Italian volcano Vesuvius erupted in the year AD 79.

▲ A glowing cloud of scorching gas and dust rolled downhill from Mt. Pelée in 1902.

Fire

▼ Molten lava spurts and flows from a Hawaiian volcano. Lava is magma that escapes from a hole or crack in the Earth's crust. Some kinds of lava flow a long way before they cool and harden into solid rock.

▲ Quiet volcanoes emit lava but little gas. The lava flows build gently sloping cones.

▲ Explosive volcanoes yield hot gas that breaks magma into ash. This builds steep-sided cones.

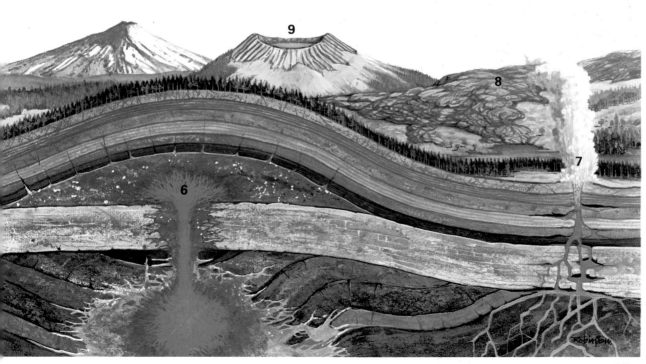

▼ These are the main currents flowing through the surface of the oceans. Others flow in other directions deeper down. Most surface currents are kept moving by the winds. But the Earth's spin makes currents veer right in the northern hemisphere, left in the southern hemisphere.

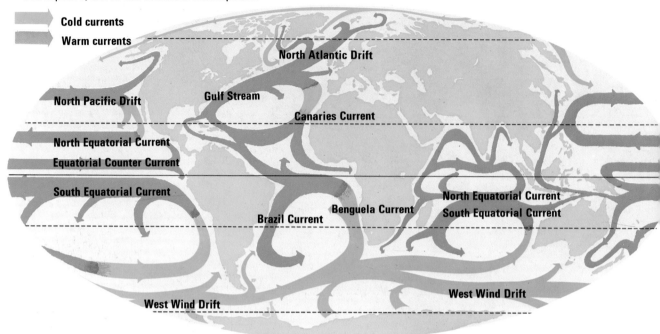

Cold currents
Warm currents

North Atlantic Drift
North Pacific Drift
Gulf Stream
Canaries Current
North Equatorial Current
Equatorial Counter Current
South Equatorial Current
Brazil Current
Benguela Current
North Equatorial Current
South Equatorial Current
West Wind Drift
West Wind Drift

▼ Wave height is measured from trough to crest; wave length from crest to crest. Each passing wave moves particles up, forward, down and back. So the water does not travel with the wave. As it circles, each water particle sets a stack of particles circling below it. In water less than half a wave-length deep the lowest particles catch on the sea-bed. This makes the waves above slow down, crowd together and pile up. Then they break upon the shore.

Spilling breaker

Plunging breaker

▲ Breakers may spill or break onto the shore.

WAVE AND CURRENT FACTS

Highest storm wave: 34 m (112 ft).

Fastest waves: 500-800 kph (300-500 mph), set off by earthquakes.

Largest ocean current: Antarctic Circumpolar Current. It carries 2200 times more water than the world's largest river pours into the sea.

Fastest ocean current: Nakwakto Rapids, off western Canada: 30 kph (18 mph).

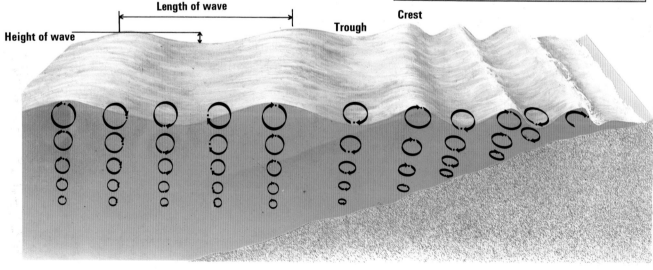

Length of wave
Height of wave
Crest
Trough

and Currents

▼A surfer speeds across the front of a huge wave moving inshore from an open ocean. Winds blowing across thousands of kilometres of unbroken sea build big waves. These rear up as they enter shallow water. This wave's crest curls forward as it slows down and breaks upon a beach.

Tides are caused by two bulges in the oceans. On one side of the Earth the Moon pulls the oceans toward it. On the other side of the Earth, the Earth's spin pushes water outward. Each day both bulges and the troughs between them, travel once around the world. The bulges bring high tides, the troughs bring low tides.

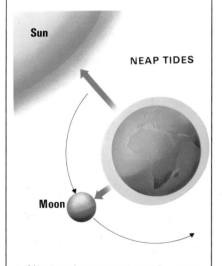

SPRING TIDES

Sun

Moon

▲ About twice a month, the Sun, the Moon and the Earth are all in line. This means the Sun's pull is added to the Moon's. Together, the Sun and Moon pull the oceans outward farther than the Moon alone can pull them. This produces extra high high tides and extra low low tides, called spring tides. Spring tides happen near the times of full moon and new moon.

NEAP TIDES

Sun

Moon

▲ About twice a month the Sun and Moon pull upon the Earth at right angles. Because they work against each other, the oceans are pulled outward only slightly. This produces lower high tides and higher low tides. Such tides are known as neap tides. Neap tides occur when the Moon is in its first and last quarters.

TIDE AND SEA LEVEL FACTS

Greatest range of tides on Earth: Bay of Fundy, Canada. A spring high tide here can be more than 16 m (53 ft) above a spring low tide.

Greatest tidal range in the British Isles: Over 12 m (40 ft) on the Severn Estuary.

Lowest tidal range: Almost nothing, at certain places in the open oceans. There are scarcely any tides in the Baltic Sea and other seas that are almost shut off from the open ocean.

Lowest inland sea: Dead Sea. Its surface is 397 m (1302 ft) below the level of the Mediterranean Sea.

A sinking city: London is slowly sinking in the clay it stands on. Engineers have had to build huge flood gates to shut out the sea.

Rising land: Some parts of Scandinavia are still rising after being squashed by ice that melted 10,000 years ago. Land on the Gulf of Bothnia rises one centimetre (0·4 inches) a year.

▼ At low tide in the Bay of Fundy fishermen pluck fishes from nets left high and dry by the receding tide. This is because here in south-east Canada there is a huge tidal range, or difference in sea level between high and low tide.

At high tide sea level may rise 16 m (53 ft) higher than at low tide. The reason is the way the Bay of Fundy narrows, and grows shallower toward its inland end. At its broad mouth the tidal range is only 2·5 m (8 ft). But the bay is funnel-shaped. So as a high tide moves up the bay it keeps on rising.

Levels

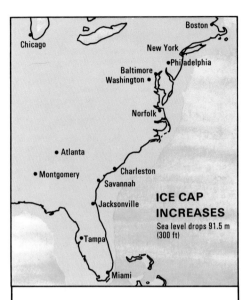

ICE CAP
INCREASES

Sea level drops 91.5 m
(300 ft)

▲ This map of the eastern United
States shows what would happen if
a new Ice Age locked up more of the
ocean water in ice. The sea level
would fall far enough to strand
many coastal cities far inland.

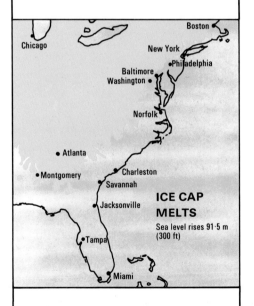

ICE CAP
MELTS

Sea level rises 91·5 m
(300 ft)

▲ If today's ice sheets melted the
sea level would rise about 90 m
(300 ft). This would drown all of the
United States' low-lying eastern
plains and their cities.

▲ The flat land above these New Zealand cliffs shows where ocean
waves once carved beaches from the coastal hills. Later, the land rose,
so these ancient beaches now stand high and dry.

There are raised beaches on many of the world's coasts. Most were
lifted by upward movements of part of the Earth's crust. But ice ages
have had similar effects: as the level of the ocean fell, old sea beaches
were left stranded.

▼ In this part of New Zealand, the sea has drowned low-lying land.
Where valleys used to lie, long, narrow strips of sea, called rias, invade
the land. Uplands have become steep-sided peninsulas that plunge
into the sea.

South-west England, south-west Ireland, and north-west France and
Spain have similar drowned uplands. The sea invades the land
because the land has sunk or the level of the sea has risen. As ice
sheets melted ten thousand years ago, the ocean level rose
everywhere, swamping many coastal lands. The rising sea cut off the
British Isles from the rest of Europe.

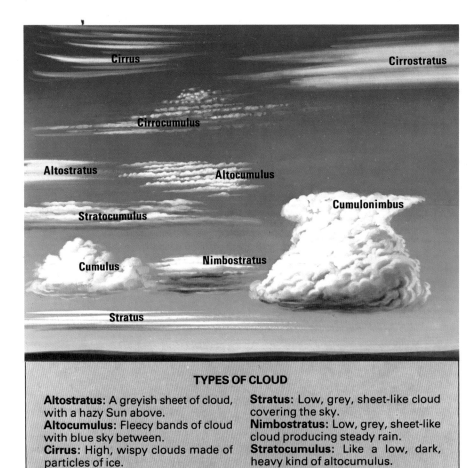

Cirrus

Cirrostratus

Cirrocumulus

Altostratus

Altocumulus

Cumulonimbus

Stratocumulus

Cumulus

Nimbostratus

Stratus

TYPES OF CLOUD

Altostratus: A greyish sheet of cloud, with a hazy Sun above.

Altocumulus: Fleecy bands of cloud with blue sky between.

Cirrus: High, wispy clouds made of particles of ice.

Cirrocumulus: Thin, high lines of cloud with rippled edges.

Cirrostratus: Milky, thin, high cloud producing a halo round the Sun.

Stratus: Low, grey, sheet-like cloud covering the sky.

Nimbostratus: Low, grey, sheet-like cloud producing steady rain.

Stratocumulus: Like a low, dark, heavy kind of altocumulus.

Cumulus: A white heaped up cloud usually seen in fair weather.

Cumulonimbus: A towering cloud that may give heavy showers.

Cold air mass

Cold front

WORLD RAINFALL

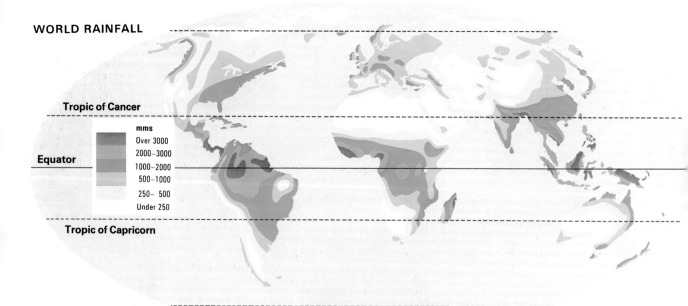

Tropic of Cancer

Equator

Tropic of Capricorn

mms
Over 3000
2000–3000
1000–2000
500–1000
250– 500
Under 250

Weather

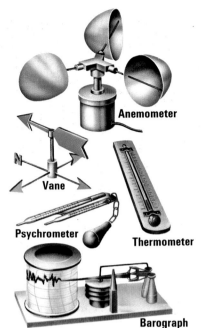

Anemometer

Vane

Psychrometer

Thermometer

Barograph

Warm air mass

Warm front

Cold air mass

MEASURING THE WEATHER

Five instruments used by weather scientists (meteorologists) for measuring the weather. **Anemometers** show wind speed. **Vanes** show wind direction. **Psychrometers** indicate humidity (the amount of moisture in the air). **Thermometers** show air temperature. **Barographs** show changes in air pressure as ups and downs in a line on a paper fixed to a revolving drum. Weather forecasters also use pictures of the world's weather beamed down from space.

▲ This diagram shows what happens in a depression, a huge circling mass of low pressure air. Beyond a warm front, warm air rises to overtake cold air. The rising warm air cools, forming clouds and drizzle. But cold air from the cold front undercuts the warm air from behind. It pushes the warm air up to form storm clouds. These will fall as heavy showers of rain or hail. Depressions bring unsettled, rainy weather. But anticyclones (masses of high pressure air) tend to give settled, usually sunny, weather.

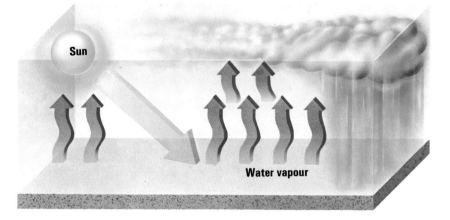

Sun

Water vapour

◄ This world map shows the depth of water falling in one year in different places. Most water falls as rain. But some falls as hail, sleet or snow. All four come from water vapour that the Sun's heat has sucked up from the surface of the Earth. Most water vapour comes from the sea.

▲ This diagram shows one of the three main ways in which rain forms. The Sun's heat warms the air and makes it rise. This air holds tiny, invisible water vapour particles. As the rising air cools, particles join to form droplets, building cumulus and cumulonimbus clouds. Inside the clouds the droplets come together to make large, heavy raindrops. These fall to Earth as *convectional* rain.

In depressions, warm air forced above cold air produces *cyclonic* rain. When an air mass rises and cools to cross a mountain range, the rain that falls is known as *orographic* rain.

Index

Acknowledgements

Photographs: page 1 Zefa; 4 Sonia Halliday; 14 Zefa; 15 Zefa; 18 G. R. Roberts *centre*, Zefa *left*; 19 Bruce Coleman *top*, Zefa *bottom*; 20 Dave Collins; 21 US Travel; 23 Pat Morris; 24 Dave Collins; 25 Zefa; 26 Australian News & Information Bureau; 27 US Travel *top*, Robert Harding Picture Library *centre*, Zefa *bottom*; 28 Zefa; 29 Bruce Coleman; 30 Robert Harding; 31 Zefa; 33 Zefa; 35 Zefa; 37 G. R. Roberts *top & bottom*.